waveforms: a short course in piano tuning

Andrea L. Hackbarth

waveforms: a short course in piano tuning
Copyright © 2025 ANDREA L. HACKBARTH
All rights reserved.

Cover art: Megan Merchant
Cover design: R.B. Simon
Interior design: Brianna Protesto
Publisher: Allison Blevins
Director: Kristiane Weeks-Rogers

WAVEFORMS: A SHORT COURSE IN PIANO TUNING
ANDREA L. HACKBARTH
ISBN 978-1-957248-44-8
Harbor Editions,
an imprint of Small Harbor Publishing

waveforms: a short course in piano tuning

Andrea L. Hackbarth

Harbor Editions
Small Harbor Publishing

*Pitiless verse? A few words tuned
and tuned and tuned and tuned.*

-Wallace Stevens

contents

prelude / 11
lessons 1-9 / 12-20
interlude: the science of aesthetic arrangement / 21-22
lessons 10-19 / 23-32
postlude / 33

waveforms: a short course in piano tuning

prelude

The first thing to understand is movement: the instrument's magic is motion and nothing more. See: the boy running & running in the afterschool wideopen, thigh muscles lengthening—contracting—lengthening. See: the murmuration of starlings rising & rising in chaotic whorl—only to converge again on the aspen tree, their warbles morphing motion into sound. The piano—just perched there—becomes all this the moment a player's fingers find the keys. Then, beneath, the ocean: waves rise up & roll their multi-particulate selves over the shore & back & up & over again (the boy imagines his toes are veiled in the receding surf; the starlings' distant cousins swoop and dive for lunch). Play a chord and the sea-god laughs at our imaginings, calling the world's whole cache of water to rise & roll & heave. Your ears, perhaps, are the shores on which the ocean breaks. You, the bare aspen branches. You, the soil compacting beneath your child's lengthening strides. You, the piano's case, so still, so stately—its purpose not containment, but release.

1.

The basic principle is this: sound is merely energy's release. A still object vibrates and lets go, sets some part of itself free. The once-hidden becomes perceptible. Imagine a church bell the moment before it is struck; now, the moment after. Recall its stillness; now witness its quickening. How it sends itself to rise & fall & rise in steady airborn cadence until the faithful—a mile in all directions—feel the gentlest of waves upon the shores of their perception and look up. I won't say that the hand of god rings the bell. But if you feel holiness echo in the bell's vibrations—the way they last & last & last beyond themselves—I will listen.

2.

Now, press a key, press two keys together, and listen. But listen: it's not the notes, per se, that ring the ears. It's the way they beat & beat & beat against themselves, against each other. The way they crash & subside & subsume one another for the briefest of moments—like incompatible lovers who can't seem to give each other up. Listen with compassion. But know that your task is structure, is objective arrangement: measure the distance each note must travel to reach the other then return again home. Sometimes you must lean in close, turn the head this way—that—to find what hides behind the obvious. Sometimes, it's like pressing fingers through the spaces between a lover's words, straining to divine what truths yet linger there. Press the keys again: softly, then again, louder. Let the dyad ring & beat & beat & then decay. Listen for a change. Sometimes, there are hints of coming storms in the length of time the leaves continue rustling after the last wind gust subsides, in the moments bridging a question and its response. Only here, you are not so powerless.

3.

Here, all power begins with the unison: the singular, the simplest of intervals. A storm is composed of so many rising waves; learn first to ride just one. Listen: a lone note laps at your ears; one key pressed and held. But look: each wave is a dance of so many particles. Look closer: one piano key can raise three wires' vibrations at once. The unison a triumvirate after all, and holy alignment now your goal. Find your shiva-state of sustain amid the constant creative destruction. Become the softly soaring dove between your distant father, your wailing infant son. But come now, this is not your soul. This is mere piano wire. This is simple physics: three wires of consistent gauge, length, and tension will vibrate at equal frequencies. And you: in control of one variable alone. Equalize their tensions and three wires will sing one unified note. Perhaps the heart strings follow forth. They say it's possible to make of yourself a single song if you balance the force among your loves, strewn here beneath the all-encompassing sky.

4.

Old sailors beneath clouded skies set their bevy of instruments before them: abacus, sextant, compass. You too have yours: a simple lever, a set of small steel tines, scraps of felt and rubber. Rudimentary perhaps, but really all you need to tame this sea of wires and waves. When the sailor aims the ship's hull just right, waves seem to cease their crashing. And you: set two wires' tensions to match and their vibrations pair and vanish. Simply learn to use your tools as you press your ears into service. Or: press your chest against the piano's storm-battered case and feel how the wires' waves converge as they meet the shore. Let your body float on them, your ears at the border of water and air. The way the salted sea enters your ear canal and all your fluid body becomes it: aim for that. A unison: sailor overboard and all in. Put down your tools and let the sea-god win for once.*

*

Once, my son and I were unison. Once, our veins sang together with one blood-born rhythm, the waters of our bodies a singular sea. We stretched motionless to every horizon. Day upon day upon day of still waters. Then: the first discordant howl of separation. Now: his being a frequency unmatched, mine a spectral echo. Here, I pull and nudge the wires till they match their mates. But the boy just runs and runs, his heart pounding & pounding & pounding on its own.

5.

Or, pick up your tools and employ the deft and delicate skill you've honed: let the unisons bloom. Who doesn't love a flower, after all? The possibility in a closed bud. The slow-moving glory-be of its opening—intentional, not accidental. The smallest of sound-wave inconsistencies can be like that. An alignment too flawless can fall flat, but the most minute mismatch creates an opening. Like the soil above the first purple crocus of spring. But you must understand: this technique is not for beginners. Wonder is greatest in anticipation, love's desire greatest in its mysterious beginnings. And that's the trouble. What you want is just the hint of bloom. But what crocus has ever stopped itself from opening full-bore to the April sun? Even knowing full well of July's soon-coming wilt. In the face of all this, you must start to develop a wiser restraint.

6.

Now do you see how difficult it is just to start? A union of this, a union of that—perfect all the unions! Maybe let them bloom—just a bit, if you can stand it. Spend hours in service of each singular note, then see if they hold. I have unified my heart with a boy and my toes with Pacific mud. My mind has settled in the still of December, while my fingers tingle with recollections of summer wind. Each of these unions a satisfaction within itself: this body a piano with 88 notes, each tuned right to its own desires. But you cannot go on like that. Your right arm will tear itself off in want of a thing your left lung cares not a whit for. Even plainsong is impossible to compose with your limbs all scattered like that.

7.

You must reign it in: pick up the pieces and compose yourself. Maybe your mother too always said as much—for propriety's sake. Listen: your first attempt at alignment will be that simple. The octave: one note and its reflection. Like this: take one wire (call it the mother for ease of recognition) and a second (the daughter) half as long. If pulled just right, when struck the daughter's strongest waves come twice as fast as the mother's. Now listen for concordance between them. Feel it: their triphasic rhythm should become a singular sparkling wave. Try not to think about the years you've spent stretching and compressing yourself in a thousand inventive ways—only to find your voice still wavering beneath hers. Try to remember: this is just piano wire; this is not your provenance. Just halve the string again & again, adjust the tension until the waves come twice again faster & faster, pitches rising in flawless spiraling waveforms. Generations of mothers and daughters echoing & echoing. Can you hear the long-forgotten matriarch? Get it right and all the world will hum in fine accord—a series of Cs or E♭s or F♯s rising in perfect alabaster columns to the open sky. What a lovely meditation. One could sit in easy peace beneath such waves. But it would not—yet—be a song.

8.

A song requires melody beyond mere repetition. The rising A your firstborn squalled at his arrival; the clear G♯ of a blue heron's mating call; the aching B♭ of a lost love's regret; the hushed D of your pencil scratch on paper—these too and all the rest must play against the mother-C. Eleven distinct tones have places to find between the octave's reflections. The question then becomes: how to help them find their rightful spots? Can you calculate the appropriate distance between the summer berry bloom and the heater's first early winter clicks? How much space should there be between your fingertips and the boy's first faltering steps? How long before regret becomes nostalgia? What tool will you use to measure these lengths when your estimates won't stop shifting? What formulas have you memorized to help with these calculations?

9.

Before you can proceed with any calculations, you must integrate one more maxim: in the singular are many. Each uttered ohm a reverence for all our echoed pleas. Each tired sigh an accumulation of all that you have lost. Listen: each pulsing vein a multitudinous song of all your selves. Remember when you held close your grieving friend and felt how her hidden veins found ways to pump in rhythm with your own? The piano's notes will do the same—if you listen well. Listen close: each note a symphony within itself; each note a whispering reservoir of higher tones. Each vibrating wire a fractalled art of divisions dividing upon themselves, all sending out their own fractured pitches. Your task: to find where the whispers align among the notes, to push and pull their wires into pleasing song. The only questions left: which notes should line up where and how? There are uncountable ways, after all, to arrange your uncountable selves. Listen: others have toiled before you; their conclusions just may help.

interlude: the science of aesthetic arrangement

a.
Pythagoras believed in the power of perfect fifths to reflect god's order. Or maybe nature's. Set one string in motion, then another, shorter—enough so that its whispered waves arrive three times for every two of the first. Set these strings to vibrate at once and you may create an opening to heaven. It really is that simple. Listen: you may hear god's voice in the convergence of these waves. And look: how easily your thumb and pinky stretch from C to G. Drop your fingers to the keys and feel the good lord's vibrations. Comprehend the ordained order of the world. Align those fifths all up and down the keyboard and you'll intuit the hum and hush of the stars. Feel the power of all this held beneath your merely human hands on ivory and wood! How we love to accept such easy perfections.

b.
Put perfection up to practicality and see which one wins out. Soon Kepler* observed that the planets orbit not in circles but in ellipses, and the perfect fell away. If the very earth can't keep a circle going round, what then of the spiraling fifths? What of the straight-stacked octaves? Pull their orbits also into ellipse form and see where that gets you. Compress & stretch & mold each interval to fit. No two waves are alike, after all. Why cling so long to unobserved ideals when the planets have been there all along, whooshing past on imperfect orbital planes? What grand celestial sound waves they must make! The musicians listened closely and found that this, too, was good enough.

*
Certainly there were more: Ancient Greece to Baroque Germany a multitudinous timespace span. Imagine: women the world over singing soft lullabies to their babes, raising strained voices to their half-believed-in gods, and humming, humming, humming to themselves. Their efforts too unlocked the mysteries of song. The women too found order, felt the universal pulsing in their breath. And yet, here we are, with these names as our guides.

c.
Newton surmised, on the other hand, that music was a rainbow pronounced. That the accurate arrangement of the musical scale should follow the way that colors space themselves on the spectrum of light. [Legend says he took a fiery poker to his own eyes in pursuit of this discovery, so it must be true.] If light comes from god, he thought—if light is god (what else could light be but god?)—we must presume that music, too, is foreordained. His logic may not hold, but a prism still twinkles and refracts. The light of pure divinity can still radiate through any mortal's dusty bedroom window. The musical scale is like that, he said. Listen: a child's fingers stumbling over his first C-major scale—the simplest one, no sharps or flats. Say it's the purest one. Can you hear the echo of god in the spaces between the notes?

d.
Whether god-light or celestial cycles guide your hands, the thing to know is this: the calculations are complex, the outcome concise. All the squabbling men approached consensus in the end: uniformity must be the aim. All eleven tones shall temper themselves equally within the octave. Measure it and you'll see: exactly 1.0595 hertz between one chromatic scale tone and the next. It's the distance between red and reddish-orange, or the force of falling stars whooshing by—smooth & bright—as your fingers climb from one note to the next. It might be like the space between your need and your desire. If you line them up just right, they say, you can have them both and still perceive the differences between. Equalize the inner drawstrings of your marrow and you too can make any song sound right. The science, after all, is there.

10.

Listen: you too can join the calculated ranks. Your task is manageable: lay the foundation for song. Don't worry yet about the singing. Simply equalize the scaletones; balance out the intervals. Memorize the work of those who've gone before you; follow the patterns they've laid out. Like this: make your thirds a fair bit wide, your fifths a little narrow of perfection, then fit the rest in tight. Even octaves need to slowly stretch their limits just a touch. No one gets exactly what they want—no simple perfect intervals—but all the songs sound okay this way. No holy purity is unattainable, but try to feel its echo pulsing through the instrument's many-layered equanimity. Follow the formula, then let yourself rise up on all the resulting equidistant songwaves. It's possible still to catch a glimpse of god, or maybe the metallic sea of Jupiter.

11.

Yet even gods and sprawling seas need reference points, and so again the question rises: where to start? (You see now how it is: starting & starting again at each new turn.) This time clarify: upon which axis does this ocean rotate? Which note will be the holy bedrock? Ask the boy and he'll say that middle C is where his lessons begin—both thumbs squeezed in there tight—so that must be the one. You too first set your fingers there; you'd be forgiven if you wanted first to right that note. But listen: you're in different territory now. Your goal now to set the foundation for his song, a task that begins a stretch beyond. So find the A above. Push & pull, stretch & contract its wires until it sends its waves to all the waiting shores exactly 440 times per second.* Take out your tuning fork to help on just this note. This is now your reference point. The child's middle-C song will follow. Remember: the origins are almost never where we start.

---

*

If you can muster blind belief in anything, make it this.

12.

Who doesn't love an origin story? We repeat & repeat the one repeated to us and build our meager lives around it. But listen: the center almost never holds. Look hard enough and every story reveals its holes. Even the A will waver & decay if you hold it long enough. Energy once released can only morph & fade. The tone cannot sustain itself at the ordained rate for long. (Can you?) And so, you must play each note again & again. Hold each just long enough to get its sense, to feel how it wants to dance. This first imprint is the important part. Just make sure it dances the same each time you press the key. Like standing alone in the dark calling *Yes Yes Yes* to the dawn, feeling how the mist-thick air absorbs your longing assent. The morning cares not for long explanations; the simple one-note *Yes* is all she needs. Say it again to make sure you believe it too. Listen: for a moment the fading A was true; that first impulse is what counts in all your calculations.

13.

To move on from that initial A requires a certain precision of calculation. Your task: find the proper placement of all the central notes. Call it setting the temperament. The piano's, that is. But first: set yours. Make firm and clear the basic nature of your being. Surely, it's not that hard. Or have you been misled by years upon years of fleeting impulses? Perhaps wandering is your tendency—your temperament a migratory bird's—yet here you are, Sunday morning, paralyzed by the weight of a small boy on your beating heart. Perhaps you've had a change of temperament. Perhaps a temperament is not so immutable after all. But again: this is a piano, not your soul. Here, you must seek stability and an even spread. Here, there are rules and procedures. There are methods of measurement. Gather your tools and set your fingers to the middle octaves: I'll show you how.

14.

Begin (again) by pressing one finger firm on your dawn-call A. Then find its reflection an octave down.* Now on that still surface, start to form your ripples. Some must spread quickly and close, like your schoolgirl heart, fluttering at the sight, at the thought, of your crush. The thirds will do that, if they're tempered right. Take the major third below your A's reflection: it should ripple at a rate of seven times per second. Can you count that fast? Can you make it exact? Can you do it again & again & one more time? This is what it takes for just one note to find its place: feel the confines of a second in your breath—and a hummingbird's wings just fluttering there, seven times. Now listen: that is just one bird. You must place a whole stack of them. The next will beat its wings nine times, the next eleven, then thirteen. And here you are: two hands insufficient to hold all these birds. One heart insufficient for all that frantic fluttering. Your lake's clear surface obscured by uncountable ripples. Too many metaphors to keep straight, while the child still keeps pulling & pulling at you. Just breathe and set the birds all to your chest: feel how their wingbeats rise in a great iridescent shimmer.

---

*
Be sure the reflection is clear. Hold your mother in the looking glass.

15.

Listen: amid the hummingbird's shimmer, you must also find the falcon's slow soar. Raise your eyes to the predator's path and let your fingers rest on the keyboard's fifths. Now count the beats just once per breath, at most. Maybe less. Maybe two long, rolling waves in three breaths' time is right. How pleasant this is, how calm, how easy. But I think you'll find it's as hard to keep your inner metronome going when the waves hesitate as when they rush. Like how hard it is to keep your path straight when cairns are too widely spaced. So easy to get lost when you can't see from one sure footing to the next. So again, it may be easier to imagine a lakeshore, imagine yourself lying there, imagine the falcon swooping from her perch. She glides softly through the haze, an occasional languid wingflap up, then slowly down again, just to keep the momentum going. Below, the lake surface ripples & ripples. The whole piano is like that—a predator chasing her prey. The heart's long held hopes chasing each day's fleeting fancies. All of it equals out to song-stuff in the end.

16.

Now you have a firm foundation, but only simple songs can rise from an equalized octave or two. Stop here and your melodies may be sweet, but they'll be small, and the piano wasn't made for such restraint. And so, your final task: spread the tempered song-stuff throughout all 88-keys. To do it right you must come back, begin again: remember the first principles of movement. Remember that vibration is the cause. Remember how it felt to set your first few strings to motion, how you reached for holy alignment, how it seemed to be there in the echoes in your ears. Remember also this: the world is not an ideal form. Here, movement is constrained. A vibrating wire's end points terminate in stiffness, while divinity floats and rings in endless endless endless echoing. But you are not as constrained as you may think: you can reach for seraphic harmonization as you work your way up and down the keyboard's length. Like this: simply stretch a bit past ideal math. Make the high notes a bit higher than you'd calculate, the lower notes the opposite. Push ever so slightly past the limits and you may find the heavenly concordance. Like holding out just a little longer than you knew you could. The way the song finally comes to you when you're already almost out of breath.

17.

In the end, though, it is not all breath and effervescent song-stuff. In the end, some grueling practicalities persist. Consider: the average piano is strung with 230 wires, bearing 45,000 pounds of tension among them. A small humpback whale can weigh as much. Imagine: the piano a young whale breached and motion-stuck in your parlor. It seems the only chance against such gravity-bound hulk is another 20-ton machine. Yet here you are—a human unadorned, armed with felt and a forearm's length of carbon fiber. Your task: to right the whale. This is where the water comes in. A whale, after all, is weightless when she has the ocean's depths beneath her. Imagine: each fiber of her muscular expanse twitching & rising with the sea's vast buoyancy. Imagine the tricks that parlor-bound beast could perform.

18.

The tuner, too, has her tricks. You, too, can learn them. Watch closely: she wraps her hand around her tuning lever, but don't be fooled—this is no delicate sitting-room handwork. Her movements appear small, mere millimeters of motion. But listen: they are magnified in shifting waves of tone. The whole sea of her body is behind it all. Waves rise up from her feet—planted firm to the floor—and churn through her bracing thighs. Tides begin in her belly and flow to her lungs, her neck, her flexing arms. Her fingers only the frothy tips of breaking waves driven by the deep-sea currents of her pelvic floor. Watch closely and you'll see: the ripples running through her to the vibrating strings & back again. The piano's song-waves wash over her, and her body replies. Soon enough, she and the whale are driven by the same distant moon.

19.

Or perhaps the piano's strings are not, in fact, the ocean or the whale, but two-hundred-thirty small, elongated moons. When livened, they pull the tides of all the room's objects. Knickknacks and dusty adornments awaken to sing their latent songs. Play a G5 and set your grandmother's portrait buzzing against the wall. A double octave of Bs rattles the dish of coins and pebbles you brought back from that trip to Venice. Remember the rainstorm? How the water curtained us on every side until we too were liquid islands. Our buoyant young selves turned dancing fish. Suddenly, a simple major third is a full-fledged song of memory sinking slowly into warming seas. And you have to decide whether that's a song you can bear to hear again. All of this requires some delicate consideration. Do you know the vibrational frequencies of each sacred object you display? What notes will bring each one to life? Are you wedded to your decorating plans? And you, with your sea-bound body, how are your waters pulled as each small moon is struck? You must remain open to the possibility that the piano has been using your tides to tune itself all along.*

---

*

Some—the old-timers—will say exactly that. Listen well enough and the piano will tell you how it wants to sing. Listen, they say, and let the soundwaves guide your hand.

postlude

At the piano there are waves and the spaces between them. And me, there, in the balance. I rest, floating in the stillness of disembodied sound I've arranged around me. I tune in to each interval, one by one. Running my fingers through final checks up and down the keyboard to be sure I've aligned them all just right. There: my child's sleeping breath. Here: my heart beat as I lie next to him. They pulse in harmonic consort. Listen: the whisper of god in the spaces between. I have given my ears, my fingers, my heart preparing all this. I await the visiting artist's master performance. But listen: there is already a song.

acknowledgments

Thanks to *Moist Poetry Journal* for first publishing "prelude."

Andrea L. Hackbarth (she/her) is a Registered Piano Technician who runs her own piano service business while also writing and editing for the *Piano Technicians Journal*. She holds an MFA in Creative Writing and Literary Arts from the University of Alaska Anchorage and received a 2022 Individual Artist Award from Alaska's Rasmuson Foundation. Her work has been published in various print and digital publications, including *Moist*, *YesPoetry*, *Lunch Ticket*, and others. She lives in Palmer, Alaska, with her son, dog, and two cats.

about Small Harbor Publishing

Small Harbor Publishing is a 501c3 nonprofit organization. Our goal is to publish unique and diverse voices. We are a feminist press, and we are committed to diversity and inclusion. We strive to bring new voices to a devoted and expanding readership.

Small Harbor Publishing began in 2018 with the first issue of *Harbor Review*. The magazine is an online space where poetry and art converse. *Harbor Review* quickly grew and now publishes reviews and runs multiple micro chapbook competitions, including the Washburn Prize and the Editor's Prize.

In July 2020, Small Harbor Publishing was officially incorporated and began Harbor Editions. Harbor Editions accepts submissions through a chapbook open reading period, a hybrid chapbook open reading period, the Marginalia Series, and the Laureate Prize.

In 2023, Harbor Anthologies began with a mission to promote texts that explore social justice issues and highlight marginalized writers.

If you would like to support Small Harbor Publishing, please visit our "About" page at smallharborpublishing.com/about.

www.ingramcontent.com/pod-product-compliance
Lightning Source LLC
Chambersburg PA
CBHW051705040426
42446CB00009B/1323